The People and the Stones

Heinz Winfried Sabais

The People and the Stones

Selected Poems
translated by
Ruth and Matthew Mead

Anvil Press Poetry

Published in 1983
by Anvil Press Poetry Ltd
69 King George Street London SE10 8PX
ISBN 0 85646 110 5
Translations and preface copyright © Ruth and Matthew Mead 1983

Printed in England
at the Arc & Throstle Press
Todmorden Lancs

This book is published
with financial assistance from
The Arts Council of Great Britain

ACKNOWLEDGEMENTS
Grateful acknowledgement is made to Frau Inge Sabais for permission
to reprint the poems which appeared in *Generation and other poems*
(Anvil Press Poetry 1968), to Eduard Roether Verlag for 'Agenda' and
'Socialist Elegy', and to J. G. Bläschke Verlag for the poems from *Self or
Saxifrage*. These poems originally appeared in *Looping über dem
Abendland*, Georg Büchner Verlag 1956; *Mitteilungen/Communications*,
© Eduard Roether Verlag 1971; *Sozialistische Elegie*, © Eduard Roether
Verlag 1975; *Selbst oder Saxifraga*, © J. G. Bläschke Verlag 1981, and
Fazit, Gesellschaft Hessischer Literaturfreunde e.V. 1982.

'A Sort of a Song' by William Carlos Williams from the *Collected Later
Poems of William Carlos Williams*, copyright 1944 by William Carlos
Williams, is reprinted by permission of New Directions Publishing
Corporation.

CONTENTS

INTRODUCTION

HEINZ WINFRIED SABAIS* was born in Breslau on 1 April 1922. During the war he was a pilot in the German air force. In 1943 he married Inge Scholtis and there were three sons of the marriage. After the war Sabais was a publisher's editor in Rudolstadt in the then Soviet Occupation Zone where in 1947 he joined a group of oppositional Social Democrats. From 1948 to 1950 he worked in the Thuringian ministry of education and acted as secretary to the committee which had charge of the celebration of the bicentenary of Goethe's birth. In 1950 he resigned from the civil service and worked in the Goethe and Schiller archive in Weimar. On 30 November 1950 he fled to West Germany where he was accorded the status of a political refugee, 'with life and limb in danger', and worked for a time as a journalist in West Berlin. In 1951 he was appointed editor of the *Neue Literarische Welt*, the journal of the Deutsche Akademie für Sprache und Dichtung in Darmstadt. In 1954 he became responsible for cultural affairs in Darmstadt. In 1963 he was elected to the city council and in 1971 elected Chief Burgomaster of Darmstadt.

A starting point in Sabais's poetry is his poem 'Looping Above the West' which conveys the sophisticated elation of the pilot and establishes the note of matter-of-fact romanticism which is typical of Sabais's poetry. The illusion of freedom in flight is worthwhile even though the pilot knows that he must return to earth which is still seen from above as a realm of possibility and the notion that 'a servant-girl conceives the new epoch' seems logical, like an imprisoning embrace. Sabais's earlier poems are poems of love and war and in the most important of them, 'Generation', he makes bold to speak for his own generation which was, it should be remembered, a generation which grew up in the echo of one war in time to fight the next. Sabais wrote elsewhere of his youth in a society suffering from mercantile impotence, politicized civil disturbance and hopelessness in many hearts. In Germany Sabais's generation experienced a return of hope only to become the second generation in succession to be used recklessly and wasted in war. Sabais reminds us that many of his generation did not survive that war and that 'those two who rot for the third' can rarely be forgotten. The experience of war has given words new associations – flowery mead/foxhole/entrenching tool; man/stomach wound/execution. The capital letter abstractions – Beauty, Love, Courage – are redefined by reference to incidents in war. The survivor cannot be

* Pronounced 'Sa-*bay*'.

certain that the past will remain the past. The present details of moneymaking and manufacture can be managed, as can the cocktails and canapés of the social round. But the present has much of an aftermath about it and there is always the feeling of being 'never quite thawed out' and the possibility of a surrealistic lapse into something which will, perhaps, never be done with. As a member of Sabais's generation I find his poem accurate. He presents the experience of that generation without self-pity, rhetoric, anger or blame. The difference between the German and the English experience is one of degree. Only two of the twenty-two members of Sabais's original squadron survived. Between 1939 and 1945 the English were, one likes to think, put out to die with a little more care than was exercised by either side on the eastern front. And it was evil things which the English were fighting against. But afterwards? One must agree with Sabais. There is no meaning, no logic, no consolation; if there is a god he is ashamed of those who function in his name. 'The rest is silence' the poem concludes. But the negations are brisk. The rhythm of the poem persists beyond its end.

Discussing the considerable influence which Anglo-American verse had had on post-war German poets, Sabais summarized that effect with the words, 'After the war we all sat down and read T. S. Eliot.' Sabais took both the epigraph to his first substantial collection of poems and the title of his last poems from William Carlos Williams' poem 'A Sort of a Song':

> Let the snake wait under
> his weed
> and the writing
> be of words, slow and quick, sharp
> to strike, quiet to wait,
> sleepless.
>
> – through metaphor to reconcile
> the people and the stones.
> Compose. (No ideas
> but in things) Invent!
> Saxifrage is my flower that splits
> the rocks.

'The political poem is a public poem' wrote Karl Krolow in a penetrating foreword to a recent selection of Sabais's poetry and prose.* Sabais was a politician, a moderate Social Democrat. He wrote a good poem about politics called 'Agenda'. It is not the

* *Fazit* (Darmstadt, 1982).

kind of poem which attempts to plot the psycho-politics of the self and the pleroma but a poem about the practice of politics by a politician in power for whom the daily burdens and challenges of office are more important than theory, who knows that any advance can only be gradual, 'millimetre by millimetre', and to whom 'ideology is just show-business'. The tone of the poem is confident, the tone of a man who knows what he is about and who is aware of the limits of his task:

> Politics
> knows no immaculate conception,
> no messiah. Politics is polygamous,
> a fertility rite in deserts . . .

We take the point, and it is the poet and not the politician who makes the point, that politics, in Williams' terms, has to reconcile the people and the stones without the benefit of metaphor. In a later poem, 'Socialist Elegy', Sabais was to defend his political moderation against the young of the extreme left. Sabais saw himself, in 1974, as a member of 'the bled-white generation' and found in the 'theory-gorged frenzy' of his opponents a recurrence of that infantile disorder first diagnosed by Lenin. Sabais knew too well the dangers of extremism and his most substantial prose work* is a record of the establishment and self-justification of tyranny throughout history and in the present. With his accustomed skill Sabais prevented his poem from lapsing into inner-party polemic or losing its way in socialist metaphysics. Sabais's position was clearly and avowedly revisionist – 'Long live Eduard Bernstein and the strict Socialist Commonwealth'.

Translating Sabais's poems with my wife over the years, and we began in 1966 with the poem 'Generation', I have on occasion been surprised to find myself writing down things which, even allowing for the ventriloquist's-dummy aspect of translation, I might have written myself. I met Sabais once. He was a handsome man.

Before his death on 11 March 1981, during the few months in which he knew he was dying, Sabais wrote a sequence of ninety poems, a selection of which is included here. The sequence spans his boyhood in Nazi Germany, street battles and burning synagogues, war in the air, days as a prisoner of war, the Russian occupation and Sabais's arrival in Darmstadt with its

> lovely hint of luck.
> Dreamt crown of a city; earnest accordance.

* *Götter Kaiser Diktatoren* (Munich, 1965).

The sequence contains his poems of death and his conceit of himself as Alcayde of Sheftheim – a village which disappeared during the Thirty Years War and of which only the name survives; and almost at the end the words, again recalling Williams, all ideas in the things always to be named:

Saxifrage on solid magma.

MATTHEW MEAD
July 1982

from Generation and Other Poems

> *Saxifrage is my flower that splits*
> *the rocks.*
>
> WILLIAM CARLOS WILLIAMS

Looping Above the West

1

Take-off. And climb. The sun
at your back, Atlas
without an earthly base, escape
into hazard, worthwhile illusion
A few optimistic stanzas
drummed on the copper woods
A fistful of engine-roar
emptied into the aquarium of mankind
The mortar-boards whipped from the heads
of the philosophers of decline – ecstasy!
Slender rocket into the last
deserts of freedom:
Drunk with the spinning horizon
Looping above the West.

2

To be I, without splintering skulls
To be I, without smashing-in ribs –
Space! The angry ardour of youth
purged in the tourney of air
in the strutting beat of three motors
through the ogling branch of crows
silver rivers as tinsel
at the edge of deliberate wings
rhythms of almost spiritual lust
arrowed at quivering cirrus and:
To be I, living my own hour –
Dream in the petrol fumes:
Embraced by the horizon
Looping above the West.

3

But startled red signals glow
on the watchful instrument panel
The hour hurtles away
The sun withers
in the yellow potato-field
A dead sky drips
on ramshackle sheds
Below in the bridal bed of hay
a servant-girl conceives
the new epoch, ephemeral lust
My time is blown away
– a little smoke in the wind:
Imprisoned by the horizon
Looping above the West.

Galley and Labyrinth

1

Burst violins
they wanted to sing noon's praises
Zenith surmounted by laughter's vitreous dome –
Now flutes lament
at distant resounding cave-mouths
where under karst
salt-water oozes away.

Pedestals empty of gods
terrible ruin
fluttering banner of sand in azure sea
a sounding star
between clouded moons which waver:
O these images, only images
stolen from lips of time . . .

2

But the wind of history arctic
from the four corners of heaven
words' withered leaves, thought's fragments
souring remains of ideas
gone down the gutter the lot
in the cross-fire of submachineguns
gone with the never explained
hardly yet conscious emotion!

Destination reached before starting
destination Desire
patrols in this Gobi of asphalt
lose themselves, never return
Coloured neuroses ringing
in minds that are helpless –
each is a foundling
none of us knowing our name.

But the storm-wind of history
rock-fall of masses
vomit, unceasing, of blood
sowing, collective, of greed
exploited depths of the sea
administered moons?
Catch as catch can
mighty Caesar
(made out of newsprint)?

Destination reached before starting
destination Desire
Neurasthenia a borehole
of cynical Poesy
a stucco of lies
and ornaments of the void
importantly stacked
in museums empty of men.

3

Ah but the man of this planet
debauch of today
cry from fires under the debris
piercing barbarian night
won't he be leaving tomorrow
to hunt notoriety?
Has he not always, evasive,
fled from his fate?

Difficult allegory man
quite inexplicable
metaphysical ABC
coding its ciphers, a self

stake and the prize
Parody or a fable?
Or a word rhyming? –
Rhyming Golgotha.

Behold the man
I, you, he:
destination Desire
Difficult allegory
thought into winds of the Arctic
Once a beam, demiurge,
arrowing into the darkness
womb evermore
tragically plagued by begetting.

4

O Ariadne
rats have gnawed through the guide-thread
no way leads to light
we are caught in the Labyrinth
words finger in vain and fumble
at shafts in the rock above us
but we are living and breathing
here in this maze of rooms!

Death and embrace will continue
each of us meet them
sometimes a triumph
in mortal, unfolding light –
Down on the beach the black ship
rots where it grounded
Galley-slaves chained to the benches
stare up the path that we took.

Generation
for Krolow

1

Jeunesse d'acier, international,
exchanging pass-words with no-one.
All the watch-fires are out, the
last logs covered with frost.
Our best cogitations dwell
in the rotted shin-bone that a peasant,
far away on the Dnieper,
far away on the Elbe,
tosses from his field, verses with
earth between the teeth,
decline without a bronze
autumn, downfall buried
by time, meaning
made obsolete by history,
no logic, no consolation,
mathematics too is no longer
valid: One was
not one but your life.
And for those who daub
him in ash upon our
foreheads, god is made ashamed.

2

Let silence rest upon
us. We read off
the text (like lovers)
from the pulsing morse
of the carotid artery
and recognize every intention
(like boxers under attack)
by the expression of the iris.

Our concepts are
sensitive and empirical.
Say: Flowery mead and we
think of fox-hole and
entrenching tools. Say:
Man – with Schiller and
Pascal – and we associate
exactly: stomach-wound, execution,
political police and all the
cunnings of self-preservation.
We do not use the words
'Passed away' when we write of
death. Our metaphors are
loaded with phosphorus.
They burn.

3

All done with? Who knows?
The hands of the clock move
around a mechanical axis,
but time strikes its hours
on our diaphragm. – Making
money, that can be
arranged, the finished product and
the brief to counsel as ordered, and
the thirty manual operations
for landing a bomber
still exactly in mind. At evening
sausages on sticks and several
cocktails, and the car waiting
outside for the carnival
of feeling to end.
Now and then the 'warmth of the nest'.
But never quite thawed out.

Steel filings in the blood and
at night the trails of nomads
crossing the brain, to the
moon? to Mars? Ah, only
a crippled gaze
follows them. And Venus
comforts with an anxiously
ready womb.

4

Jeunesse d'acier, slowly
eaten by rust, Roland,
whom they omitted to kill,
now in retirement. At twenty
led attacks, commanded
U-boats, aimed bombs.
At thirty veterans, collecting
administrative experience, and
studying the laws of natural
corruption almost with
indifference. No blow
is so strong that it shakes
the centre where the unrecountable
dream dwells – which doesn't
help. Sometimes in a
frivolous mood or
in re-won folly
we forget those two who
rot for the third.
But otherwise optimism remains
a symptom of old age, too
early for us, too childish.
The white blocks of new
bazaars, nickel and chrome,
are only a seduction
of the retina, progress is

pulped newspaper, the chambers
of the heart are leaded and
the dust of already re-utilized
debris will lie long
on our lids.

5

But: Beauty, Love, Courage?
No, only the torment of traumatic
revisions which are without
significance in philosophy!
That was Beauty: a
sunrise. We parachuted
down on the bridgehead. The
machineguns pointed upward. Sunrise.
And Love: Pale faces
which one strove to face in silence
or a willing body and
thirty minutes. Luck too:
amputation was not necessary.
Art: when one banked
steeply enough to get out of
the line of fire. Honour:
exchanged for bread while a
prisoner-of-war or deleted for the sake
of strange outrages. Courage:
sold as a job lot during third degree.
The Inner Life: very decimated
and disowned; for the old shamans,
specialists in the psyche, mix new
and effective poisons. But: Peace?
Frieden? *Pace*? – the weapons
are brought up to date.
And Truth is: the lie
which we love.

6

Jeunesse d'acier, generation
without youth, without age, a
cracked bell in the head,
discord in the pleasant peal
of antique ideas. No specimen.
Wordless drama. Had they
nothing to till? – Graveyards!
And the historical achievement?
So-and-so many million fallen.
What that is, is known here and there –
to an old woman who has
no more tears, to a pensioner
who studies the atlas because
a strange place-name will
not come to mind, to a child
who is shown a yellowing
photograph: That was
your father. Later, perhaps,
a dilettante, questioning history,
will find: Their wordlessness was
an Odyssey, two thousand years
after Christ, when concentration camps,
boycott and the hydrogen bomb
were invented. The rest
is silence.

Radio Message

Entrench your heart.
The wolf-packs prowl.
A shepherd in the Beskids
found a flock of doves frozen to death.
A factory on the Volga
has more than doubled
the production of handcuffs.
Entrench your heart.

Outwit your wrath.
Automatic eyes follow
the course of every cloud
across your face.
Men with machine-heads
demand in punched-card language
a justification of your dreams.
Outwit your wrath.

Cast off your hope.
Those well-meaning gentlemen
who nodded to you in the studio
cannot shoot.
Only death stands at your side
and controls your every movement
with the stop-watch.
Cast off your hope.

Conceal, at once, your thoughts
– most dangerous ammunition – beneath time,
a cocked verse in the reading-book
of your son, lament and pain
in the sounding-board of a violin.
And trust the law: the invisible
weapons of freedom
are also deadly.

Political Printed Matter

Be of good cheer, you oppressed and desperate:
Every Bastille yet has been stormed,
Every tyrant lay at last in the dust.
Nothing remained of the governing lies
But the boundless laughter of history.

Be of good cheer; some morning will again be
the fourteenth of July. Reason will
distribute her weapons to the insurgents,
and the agents of oppression
suffocate from their own unscrupulousness.

Be of good cheer: ten divisions armoured
with blindness can perhaps crush your
rights, but the idea that is true
remains in all awakened minds.
It surrounds power and will disarm it.

Be of good cheer: what you believe in, what is right,
becomes freedom. She destroys the officially
controlled fallacies. She lays the bomb
beneath the dictator's map-table. She
works silently for the just society.

Be certain: the step of freedom is as sure
as the course of the sun. She hands on her
binding passion through the stream of generations
and enacts, when it is time, the law
which determines anew the dignity of man.

Chanson d'Amour

The lonely birds of the night
The gentle rattle of stars
in the flute-play of your eyes
My foolish word
Germaine.

Four walls of blood-red glass
The gloomy spiral of stairs
Your growling dog at the gate
I think, but you love.

The bed where we lay flecked with phosphorus
(Woebegone German carnations
under Napoleon's pondering gaze)
How amorous was our blood!

And already the kiss is freezing
at which the weapons are pointed
The sad snow of the street-lamp
covers your hair, my breast.

We, tiny hollow of feeling
carved into the stone of history
To be covered with dust tomorrow
Who will find the place then
Germaine?

Arctic Hour

Arctic hour
icy snow
in the veins: I
call to the infra-red
midnight sun
You, light-years from here,
beloved in the burning
bush, ask the
bleaching Sphinx
for rain.

Between us only this
frayed meridian
of hope to which
continents cling, between
us strange eyes
which we have drunk
dry, hands ringed
with our most forgotten
gazes and this
hopeless epidemic
of mankind. But our
dead angels drift
over our heads
into entropic space.

Why did you
know my blood?
Why did I
hear your heart?
Arctic hour
in which a decade
freezes, bush
in which my love
burns: *E non ci*
indurre in tentazione
ma liberaci dal male.

Melancholy

Melancholy
your sun is black
your sea has stony waves
the flights of your gulls rattle
like strokes of the scythe
through my heart
I no longer see a coast.

And on the shore of memory too
only your track
down to the tide-line
The bog-water
before my door
is my mirror
Ah, time vanishes
from my sight
some death besieges
me within
I would
that I were lost.

But behind the earth-shadow
of your brows
is it her glance?
Even in your hissing
attack I hear
the breath of her love
Yes, she is there
before the icy pane
a breath
and a release
I am
to forget myself.

Myth

I wanted to devise an Orient
of words for your eyes
I let my joy blaze up
round you like camp-fires. In vain!

I meet betrayal
in the first word
Every second-hand hacks
angrily into our world
which will never be
and this chilly south
which kisses us
casts only dry seeds
from the tree.

I saw a sunset
on your lips, saw it
wordlessly. Never again!
Tomorrow perhaps a stony Venus
in whom I do not recognize you
will smile at me
in a deserted gallery.

Dream-Fern

This evening in May, Asiatic death
in the heart! A moment of confusion
draws back the bolt of glass
Speak softly or gorgon eyes
will steal time from our words
Stay close, skin to skin,
there is so much distance beneath
the lids. See, your shoulders are white
like aluminium, ah, lit only by the murderous
blossom of fleeting hope
and the blind ruby of your lips
describes a mouth of shadows.

Do not take fright when the roll of drums
beating farewell breaks against the doors
and obliterates the bewildered
sonata of hand and thigh
Only I have to go, you can sleep
alone, night-roses, dream-fern –
this bouquet of kisses
engendered by our breath will remain here
and as you sleep I shall place
the wild thistle of our youth
in your greying hair.

This evening in May, and the flight
back across Acheron, the blade of
moon at my nape. Behind me
the cement curtain of the city fell
but beneath the stones
our nightingale still sings, you hear it –
and as Venus pales my blood flows
into the fjord of your dream
Day hesitates on the east, chilly
and rock-grey. Soon I shall lie again
stiff in the arms of the wall
where, yesterday, I was shot.

Iphigenia of Bochum

In the midst of this breathless epoch
in the panorama of shrapnel-scarred asphalt
antiquity a little careworn, cool jazz
and lilac smile of filmstars
in the midst of neon-pale prosperity
confronting bar-sniggers and newspapers
here among thieves and accountants
as inspiring as buried cries
in the ruins: a face
a brow, almost unravaged
Iphigenia of Bochum.

Troy and Thule in the grey eyes
eyes which made submachineguns
useless, eyes which kissed the hunted moon
through the military hospital window
when no air-raid warning fell from the sky
eyes, knowing, stirring imagination
eyes like symbols: a cross deep
in the iris and the small yearning
for avenues where there was perhaps
a last gesture: Hector went
columns of tanks. Gone.

On the lips the forgotten song
lovely desire and the question
for which there is no new word as yet
lips carved in steel, prelude
taken up by the curve of the hips
a theme for Bach, with the grace
of French goddesses
lips of timeless love –
But too fleetingly touched
but too purely desired:
Iphigenia of Bochum.

Lyrical Variation on Pointless Moments

I was snow
lovely geometry
spoken softly against your brow
on a faint-hearted evening –
you felt nothing.

I was stone
in the long gutter
of yesterday's failures
I traced the wavering stenography
of your track into antiquity –
you did not see me.

I was sound
a Gershwin staccato
a turbine's elegy
Ah, only the whir of
a humming-bird's wing behind glass –
you were deaf.

I was a thought
between two pulls at an Havana
burnt into the curtain of the meaningless
day, a compass-needle quivered
slightly in your eye –
I was not your thought.

I am the man
whom you forgot to expect
You look at my shoulders
Your buried love blushes
Quickly you spell out the empty morse signals
into my old wordlessness
Only one denied gesture divides us –
I passed by.

Anagram

Nothing can trouble
the eucharist of our eyes
Bengal lights swim
in our blood

A white aviso glides
through my expectation
Your breath shoos the Erinyes
from my track –
Enchanting as Goethe's prose
the dispensation of our hearts
their impatient rhythm
tambourine and shawm

When the soaring crane of fate
ploughs the horizon
our dream will drift
past the Delphic rock.

Eros

As I went from you
your scent on my neck
the weary streets
stuck lanterns in their hair
and the birches
cast their whitest shadows
before my feet.

In my blood
the smoke-soft contours
of your face, which I
trace at midnight on the brow
of the moon as comets in love
whizz round her.

In my blood
impatient sails, rattle of weapons
the Argo's voyage to salt-feathered
archipelagos, wild cry of cranes
at the bow, and the lungs
full of the smell of burning.

In my blood
the Elmo's fire of your shoulders
the swift hyperbole
of this fierce passion
and the lily-coolness of fingers
on the throbbing temples.

In my blood
squadrons in formation, radio signals
from Pole to Pole, cyphers
of death over darkened cities
and the smile of Venus, far
far above the bomb-sight.

In my blood
compelling as the guitar-voiced
poppy in July, the law
of your womb – which I
shall brand into the Place de la Concorde
with the wing-feather of Gabriel.

In my blood
the grinding negation
of time. Lonely prayer
hoisted from the minaret. The priest
raises the Host. At the last
three handfuls of earth, for you and for me.

In my blood
gleam of moss, reed-shawm
The meadows of Mars bloom
with earthly love
Your kisses, a flight of doves,
besiege the shimmering
pinnacles of Utopia.

In my blood
Siberian tundra, wolf-packs,
powdery snow on nomadic tents,
forced-labour brigades struggle
with shivering fir trees. Ah, inescapable
exile, nailed by shots
behind the edge of the forests.

As I went from you
your scent on my neck
the weary streets
stuck lanterns in their hair
and the night
laid my racing heart
to the lips of the sky.

Snowfall

Snowfall of words
Snowfall of wishes
Snowfall of hours –
Quiet statistics of our futility.

Gentle fires still burn
in the ante-chambers of the heart
Drunken lilies would like
their patience to flower to its end
But with jagged shadows ahead
farewell echoes roughly already
through the tunnel of the veins.

Here one moment, gone the next
my Icarus 'Swissair Munich-Milan'
which flung the roaring breadth
of its wings around our hips
and its good-natured distance
about our temples. Now as before
naked and alone again.

Was not the luminous dial,
vampire at your wrist, driven off
by the sweetest salvo of earth?
Now, from the abstract ambush,
the old rusty numbers hiss
again in our ears
and we listen.

Your eyes are locked tight
medallions which abduct an image
Estranging light reddens
the hair at your nape. The hard-edged
look of morning has
grazed your mouth
and the last imagined kisses
crumble like sand from your lips.

No I. No you.
The cry of crows
squats on my petrified shoulder
Who will find my lost language?
A caterpillar of snow
spins a cocoon for my hair
Who walked away on my feet?
tears of fright in ashamed pores
Who takes my body from me?

Behind the curtain: Monday
Bored it aims at us
the ticking weapon
but our limbs have broken off
their conversation. Our memories part
coolly and at variance.
The minute-hand of the airport clock
drives us apart, nervous,
there is no time to suffer farewell
like a last farewell.

Snowfall of words
Snowfall of wishes
Snowfall of hours –
Quiet statistics of our futility.

Shall We Meet Again

Shall we meet again
in the wordless wastes beyond us
where caravans of the dead are travelling
uncertainly towards the Oasis
Nowhere or God?

Shall I still know your name
when the body's memory
flakes cruelly away and your image
is extinguished as my
last thoughts break apart?

Shall I still keep your love
where the edge of the great shadow
strikes me and numbs the sweet unrest
What will remain once eternity's
hate melts the foolish flesh?

Who will lend us eyes for each other
in the laconic solemnity of nothing
when the wave of earthly time freezes
glassy before our feet
and no desire moves it?

Shall we meet again
in the wordless wastes beyond us
in the swaying shadows of uncertain caravans
in the Oasis Nowhere or God
deep in untimely snow?

Agenda

Agenda
for Hensel

1

Ikebana of sensitively attuned
words, resultless delight
of late drawing-rooms – or Hölderlin's
swansong, heartbreaking, where enough
understanding might be felt?
Schri, Kunst, schri! Goethe said
to be a writer is no
profession. A civil servant: built roads,
designed equipment for the Corps of Hussars,
took care of the fire service, thought
of mining when he thought of Ilmenau
and enjoyed love and beauty
in the intervals of very prosaic business.
Max Frisch ought to have been
a mayor *à la* Montaigne.
Mao created a state and buried
freedom in his poem.

2

Life is lived in states,
in cities. One dwells better and
more fleetingly in books. Time is
what does not return, owed
to oneself and others. Assume
the burdens of necessity,
try, bemused, to smile, to think,
to act for a man in despair and
you will know who you are. Put
the day's trivia through the
chaff-cutter of logic

and sieve out the profit,
to be shared by many. For the daily
toad insists on being swallowed
imperturbably. Only the Pope
is infallible. And he
prophesies out of very old books.

3

The day drawn up like an
estimate of costs. Statistics
of difficulties, prognosis
of effects. Your own life
cut into slices, everyone
helps himself: This is my body,
this is my blood. – And this
my anger, my scorn and
my compassion. The good man,
the evil man of Sezuan,
superhuman burden. How many
faces in which thoughts
have to be kindled!
In each a Mozart or
a Himmler. To shoot
distant stars with the most subtle
instruments and to wade in the swamp
across sleeping crocodiles.
World, your king is
Augeas and Hercules was
a rumour not to be repeated. Here
other volunteers are required.
Send for Sisyphus!

4

Ridiculous to hope for fame,
for gratitude – what are they? Better
a few drinks with friends
after the great sigh of relief, when
the books balance, the funds
suffice, collective labours
succeed and they storm the
new school, pathetic penguins,
with sharp beaks, the candy-sugar
comet of Bethlehem on their side. – Yes,
this is the stage which is the world.
How green was my valley, Neanderthal,
How blue were the skies. And
ask of art my ever-due
catharsis. I know
it is essential.

5

To escape occasionally, to flee
the telephone, out of the
hectic mass-masturbation.
To read aphorisms between two
conferences, poems on the
lavatory. Or to admire trees
and their natural consistency,
of which Brecht knew nothing.
And to greet roses without
pressing them into metaphors. To ignore
with sympathy the couple in the grass.
To inspect buildings under construction
sobers you up. To reflect upon
the difference between H_2O and water,
upon the jaunty anti-Leninism

of the Brezhnev doctrine, about horses
a bit. To make notes
about stupidity and fanaticism.
To find criteria against contentment.
To explain to your son
the pleasures of poetry and mathematics.
To buy tobacco and paperbacks,
chocolate for the woman you love.
To travel by tram, gossiping
with people. To lie on the beach and
think of nothing, with the sun
and a cigar full in your face.

6

To advance, millimetre by millimetre,
ideology is just show-business.
A thousand-voiced reality needs
a thousand and one clear answers. So file
away the dead-sure system. Theory
is like a film, has a beginning, an end –
everything else flows. Politics
knows no immaculate conception,
no messiah. Politics is polygamous,
a fertility rite in deserts,
in the jungle, above volcanoes.
I too have surveyed my utopia
and like to chart the prospects,
– forget it, humanity comes in
through this door, sits
here on this chair, give at once,
or your heart is made of paper.

7

To advance by millimetres. The files
on the desk. I know, they need
another threepence an hour, bathrooms,
better schools, and they'll
want culture. They need co-determination,
and they will learn to abhor dictators.
What use are the eye-rolling quotations
from the day before yesterday, the romantic
heroic poses? My father was a worker,
I learnt politics from him. He rated
the inventor of the electric light bulb higher
than Liebknecht, whom he worshipped.
To say what is, to make what should be –
I preferred what he said to
organ music and sermon. The theory,
he said, is quite simple: oppression
causes barbarism, exploitation causes poverty.
There are no gods among men,
no once and for all, no paradise
here or anywhere. Progress means
work. Sense comes from understanding,
grasp from a grip on things. Try it
out yourself. Thus my father.

8

Young men, why do you borrow the beards
and top-boots of your great-grandfathers?
Have you no heads and feet of your own?
Fathers depart, you arrive. Be original
and the game will belong to you. Sure,
we only back certainties. Why?
We have children. We use dreams
as hypotheses. Illusions
make us bitter and impatient.

If you want to feel the creeps take a
look into your own guts sometime. And
then at our Stalins and Hitlers.
That didn't just make history,
it lies in the chromosome, and
in you too. Horizons of faith are
always cloudy, you'd be better employed
paving roads. What do you want to climb on
if not upon our shoulders?
Look outside, the windows are
open, even though no
picture-book sun shines in. Our
allergy to bars and barbed wire
is not the worst inheritance.

9

History in millimetres –
the total order is
the total lie. No one however
grants us what endures. We do not endure.
Each night the test of non-
return, each day that comes
a sensation. The clocks are wound up
for tomorrow. Now to breathe garden air,
to follow the flight of the swallow without envy,
to lick the day's wounds,
to read a bit. Or tenderness,
kisses, lust. Wordless exchange of happiness.
Happiness, loveliest coincidence, indispensable
art. To be announced in each item
of the agenda. And for me too
at the latest under 'Any other business'.

1970

Socialist Elegy

Socialist Elegy

> . . . and there would be nothing left
> to us but to bewail our state of slavery.
> *Solzhenitsyn*

1

We, born in back-street slums,
in the days of the proletariat;
narrowness, constraint, a stable warmth without
share capital, interest-free,
human material meant
for immediate consumption: learning
in order to be of use; culture
amuses the gentry. Trained
from first youth for the mass grave. Nevertheless,
despite knee bends, despite humiliations,
self-determination from within,
cajoled pleasure, my
cajoled life, be as
it may, my life!
Let a thousand flowers, a thousand
obscene curses blossom above the
murderous collectivisms
of this wretched century!
Fascism, communism and
so on forever, *merde*, no thanks!
The parliamentary foot in the door
to all power and, nicely calculated,
social legislation in the till!
And the Rights of Man
nowhere lost sight of
for a moment.
The dignity of man,
mine, yours, his, hers,
ours, yours, theirs, always

taken concretely and
given too, outmoded measure
of that not to be relinquished:
better to die than crawl.

2

That would have been that then:
Marching orders straight
across Europe. To kill
or be killed.
Hunched solidarity
with those who suffered.
Melancholy amid bloody vomit
and lies and hate.
Montaigne in the knapsack,
that endured. Educated
by retreats, fleeing
from victory to victory. The
lesson of our lives:
The senseless
machinery of might,
greased with degenerate
ideals. Optimism was
betrayal of your neighbour. The cleverest
technique of survival:
To abandon everything, let go,
lose, in order to keep
yourself. Moments
alone, with two or three gathered
together, never more. The sum total:
Systemized happiness is organized
misery, the unspoiled world
a crematorium-dream.
Nothing is worth it, nothing, nothing at all,
to kill, to let yourself be killed.
This as experience.

3

That would have been that then:
Surviving with effort
both the Brown and Red
benefactors of mankind. Clearing
rubble, starving,
begging. Marriage, work,
discovering duties, coddling
the offspring, writing
books for no one, helping
to built new cities, practice.
Reason too – holding high
the gay and free in muck
and luck. No line, certainly, only
the erratic succession of very
individual points in approximation.
But history is not designed for you
nor for a single generation.
You have only your
lifetime, one lifetime, and
you realize that very slowly.
Little enough, acquired:
books, pictures, enough to live on
for a year and too much
moral surplus,
not to be consumed by moods.
An unconcern with real estate –
never be static. One
must be able to withdraw,
now, always. Off into the
woods, grey-head, get away
when the lemmings come.
To be free as a bird,
prepared in the end
to be an outlaw, the one thing
that costs nothing, at most
your head.

4

The generation that is, that will have been:
the bled-white generation,
squashed, historically, between
tyrannical fathers
('Gott mit uns!')
and fanaticized grandsons
(Marx mit uns!)
theory-gorged frenzy,
which wants simple totality
instead of difficult truth,
madly rebreeds its own stupidity –
to the nuclear *éclat!*
We are still here, cool as autumn,
the sceptical coolies,
shall soon be gone.
And now abideth:
Fugitive trace elements
of humanity in this
and that for a while;
soon a manipulated saga,
a counterfeit smile
in the social concrete, finally
wastepaper, nothing, nothing at all.

5

Poke fun at yourselves,
Epigoni, sheep in wolves' clothing,
on your noisy march
from concentration camp to concentration camp.
Know-it-alls, know-nothings!
In all perfect systems –
believed, thought-out –
inquisition breeds.
Your closed image of the world,
a penitentiary: a relapse into

'self-induced infancy'.
Many doors are open to fools,
no exit; there are only
escape routes over the wall.
Stalin in Marx,
like the doll inside the doll.
Do you want to dance
again the bestial dance
of death? Why? What for?
Another GULAG society?
Long live Eduard Bernstein
and the strict Socialist Commonwealth!
That requires work,
however, not opium.
Sweat out, lemmings, what
you have learned by heart,
the intoxicating illusion!
Your Mayakovskys praise
murder – with suicide
already in their skulls.
Your revolution will
devour you (big eats!)
like hot fish-fingers.
The frost of your fire, you can do it,
will glaciate Europe, or
with luck (furtively)
you will escape yourselves.

6

May our dust in that day
lie light upon you,
a useful hacking cough
for your computers. And
an ancient nuisance
to your Chinese bosses.

1974

from Self or Saxifrage

1

I write the birches, the house
and the river, this place was mine.
Here as a child
I planted my lilac bushes.
Grandmother prayed out loud
as grandfather lifted me
laughing on to the horse: My little
blonde Tartar, he shouted.
The house burned but
the lilac blooms. For passers-by.

3

The cherry trees lining the road to Leuthen
stood on land my grandfather leased. We stayed
there in a hut in summer with our dogs
scaring away the starlings and picking cherries.
To the south loomed Zobten, the sacred hill,
where herds of cloud grazed slowly towards the east.
Potatoes grew over the soldiers' graves.
A cool breeze came from the woods near the Oder.
In the old chestnut tree on the hill
I sat and sang and the birds listened.

5

Black Uncle Bolko, the coal merchant,
smelled pungently of horses, old Polish
nobility and gin. When we had stabled
and curried the horses and fed them their oats
we washed the coaldust from our faces
and went to Grabolle. The card-school
sat round the scrubbed white wooden table,
the cards were shuffled and dealt.
In between there was Cracow sausage
and plenty of beer to drink.
Eighteen, Twenty, Two, your lead. At midnight,
I carried the lantern, we swayed home singing.

9

I received my baptism of fire in the ancient manner
at my father's side in a streetfight
between the Browns and Reds. We lay in the entrance
to a coal-cellar opposite their headquarters pub.
Windows shattered above our heads, they were shooting.
Hand-grenades now, said my father (Third Regiment
    of Footguards).
The police reassembled the republic.
Legality, yes, there ought to be legality. Law for all.
But soon force was stronger, our spirits sank.
Did not want to sacrifice ourselves and were sacrificed.

19

The synagogue burns. Its Meneketel
inscribes the brows of the startled multitude.
Who will preserve your house if the house of God
    is burning?
What are you worth if certain other men,
placard around the neck, are maltreated?
If they are robbed and murdered by the state today
you could be robbed and murdered by the state tomorrow.
November thirty-eight. And I hear my father
whisper from behind his newspaper:
From now on, son, it's every man for himself.

22

Almost before confusedly you have found her
    you are chosen.
Paradise is reopened for you, a labyrinth.
The demiurge casts its spell of fertility.
Delights of unexceeded beauty are possible.
And repeatable, when certain forms of organization
are established. A part of that oceanic
feeling requires rationalization. Domesticity
and child raising cannot be left to chance
or achieved lying down. She knows that.
You are the bizarre bird, start singing!

27

The red cracked lips
of my beloved, my wife, and
the touching bundle beside her
with eyes, nose, mouth – our child.
My senses were still blunt
with the noise of battle,
sweat of fear, smell of death;
then came that light,
a tiny star in the midst
of barbarism, alpha and omega.

28

In the clattering hollow of night with labouring clouds,
something without mercy coils around your throat.
Your brain a lump of ice stringing together
frozen code-numbers; squadron turn on to target.
Destruction is steered now by mechanical commands.
Hit aircraft dive like torches. In the vortex
of flame the white faces of friends on fire.
Hot metal rips cold metal. The hiss of carpet-bombing.
Moloch casts himself suddenly over the edge of the earth.
You have fulfilled your function, my hero, reliable
    clockwork.

32

Berlin burning at evening. The megalomaniac
has condemned himself. Four of us, armed, westwards.
Greening fields and humming heath. The wood like
   the Good Lord.
Armoured artillery in the distance, machineguns
of low-flying Lightnings close at hand. At night snorting
knots of cavalry, shouts in Russian, a salvo.
Pressed close to the webbed roots we exhale death.
Touch the cold iron, drunk with the scent of pines.
In the grey dawn across the Elbe, identity discs round
   our necks.
Report to the cookhouse, said the negro sergeant.

34

Gnawed roots and grass in Kreuznach
in the open field of the PoW camp.
Gnawed disgrace and scorn
for the crimes of the Brown fanatics.
Gnawed the bitter lessons of world history
marked on our brows with blood and shit.
Gnawed the last stale illusions
and left them behind in the latrines.
Looked with indifference through the barbed wire:
There flows our river Comrade Heraclitus.

36

The coat of the teacher killed at Stalingrad fitted.
His widow would have gladly given more; I only
needed books. Goethe was in the bookcase.
Machorka between my lips and swedes in my knapsack
it was easy to bear all the Caudine yokes.
High Heidecksburg where I wrote stories for the annuals
and my tobacco plants rampaged over the balcony.
There the Saale flashes and my fishing-rod flashes too.
And there where Prince Louis Ferdinand died like a dolt
I stole potatoes at night for my hungry children.

38

Became political as the future was nothing
but hunger, patience, clearing rubble.
Wanted to work with facts, do something practical.
The Soviet commander explained the Stalin constitution.
I was responsible for the supply of firewood.
Was parish councillor, freely elected to unpaid office.
As the Social Democrats were forcibly cut down
to Communists I went over to the Liberals.
Remained an incorrigible revisionist *à la* Bernstein.
Politics is working with facts, is work, creates facts.

39

They need land and cattle, the refugee peasants.
The great estates are divided up among them.
The revolution is on the march, announces the district
    president.
The old Baroness is shut up in the cellar.
The castle at Gross Kochberg is open to looters.
But the Soviet power allows no spontaneous pranks.
It knows after all about Goethe and Frau von Stein.
So the surly revolutionaries load the books
and Goethe's desk and the old Baroness as well
on to our army lorry. And leave the castle in peace.

42

We slept on straw in the railway station waiting room.
It was our first night in that horribly disfigured city
which promised to be our new home. Debris and rats,
    grey dust
at dawn. In the market a despairing assembly.
But on the Mathildenhöhe a world summer-ripe:
Van Gogh oaks in gardens drunk with colour,
golden cupolas and fantastic artefacts.
We who had slept on the floor smelling of poverty
breathed new peace, the lovely hint of luck.
Dreamt crown of the city; earnest accordance.

43

You mustn't kowtow to anyone,
she said, you mustn't let
anyone humiliate you
for our sake, she said,
it's true we've no money
but resign anyway,
turn it all in, your
children and I, we need
no lackey. We have no talent
for cringing, we shall manage.

44

As they laid upon me
the gold chain of office and I
saw the resignation in my
predecessor's eyes, I felt
the chill of history:
Expect no gratitude and be thankful
when you reap no ingratitude –
I am not too bad
to fail, not too good
to be of use, I said.

46

Our children, beings imperfect as we are.
Good, there are your eyes, your brow, your gait.
All too similar ways of speaking are being ironically
    scored.
Shallows are easy to forgive. But the strangeness?
These dark repellent eddies, where do they come from
wanting to make a name of their own, a face of their own?
Leave the options open, to be free to depart is freedom.
And do not expect gratitude, give even more lavishly.
Your assurance at least must be gratis.
They will see who you are, who you were, your children.

59

He looked almost worried
and suddenly pulled my ear:
'Do you have to die now?'
'Perhaps, who knows' I
replied. 'No' insisted my grandson,
that little bundle of energy
that couldn't yet read or write,
'I want you to tell me
a story!' 'Which
story?' 'Hans in Luck!'

60

Acropolis, plaything for sun and moon,
charms conserved-to-death, 'commercialized to the end'.
Understand the darker mythology of your own belly.
Where is the spirit of that world? Beauty
as harmony with the gods; gone.
Were the ancients surer than we of their idea?
All this came from Zeus and Zeus is dead.
Beneath the negating ray from today to Ur
will the cosmos end lumped into iron?
The next god, Pythia, would have to invent himself.

64

They brought the thornbush here from the Cevennes.
Barricades for the Waldenser mountain villages:
No oath, no tithe, no military service.
No hierarchy and the right to speak among equals.
In the thornbush the Holy Ghost burnt on bloody earth.
Cattle prospered on the mountain pastures, vineyards
    in the valley.
Force drove them out, the thornbush blossomed
beneath the bear of Berne till they had to depart
    once more.
Bred horses in Prussia and Poland. Here
stood the house of my fathers: ruin and thorns.

74

When read almost all is explicable;
not death. Imagine friends smelling
the corpse, tear-racked farewell.
And understand Golgotha, understand religion
and the veil of art. Symbols,
swaying and imprecise, perform.
O unquenchable curiosity about darknesses,
about solar systems within me which are real,
about the daily provocation of the facts.
I'm busy, love, involved in living.

76

Why fix your stare on dogma, look inwards.
No candle flicker but the starry universe
is our homeland. Lose limits, passer-by,
in meditation, in music, let go.
Beginning and end become one.
Time moves through you lightly
and loses itself beyond the horizon.
You will not stay here. You are.
Endure all you know too well until
you are taken back into the numinous.

79

History, you know, history happens to you.
The school taught the tale of heroes.
Woe to the defeated, the rubbish
of history, without justice.
The earth is full of crusted blood.
The master who called me a dunce
because I took Hector not Achilles
to be Homer's hero – how did he die?
The gods live on human flesh. Behold:
a man, a bundle of fear and courage, I.

82

We know for certain that nothing at last ends well.
All the graveyards are overcrowded with future.
Man, a cloud of dust in the wind, driven
a while by frustration and desire, then perishing.
Moloch world, cannibal from the start,
who shall change it, the young cannibals?
Religion and enlightenment: melancholy games which
never reach conclusion. My murderous Auschwitz-century
can still be surpassed. Moloch is perfecting
his technique. Then say why you go on living? Because.

83

Friendship, to be like each other and to enjoy
the contrasts, that darkens and turns to lustrous gold
like an old blessing handed on in family icons.
Rivers join, mountains are moved.
My tongue is twofold. Darknesses flee away
in this moment. Several galaxies are at my disposal.
The riddles of the world seem to have solutions.
Living in this lion's den, back to back.
Cain and Abel only brothers, fuddled with the smoke
of sacrifice. Our triumph: the grace with which the sparks
    fall into nothing.

85

That we must all 'straddling the grave'
be born like the beasts
ought to make us humble, but we forget.
What kith and kin can make of us
we know: broken limbs, tortured
flesh, cringing greed, a heap of decay.
The good deed, the greatest, done without
ostentation does not count. We must die
in greater agony than our cattle. Misery
at the beginning. Calamity at the end. Now smile.

86

The shadow strikes deep. You are a marked man.
Faces do their best: bewildering pity.
And turn away to follow their own objectives.
You are out of the race, only your horse is still running.
Find a thicket to hide in; the sight of you is unnerving.
A smell of wreaths. Doctors ration your life.
You see in the brooding eyes of those who love you
what you are meant to be here from now on:
You pass away as a lovely day of remembrance.

87

Where the scent of fir trees meets you,
the brook paints patterns in its bed,
the buzzards circle around you
and the meadows overflow with green,
there you will find me in an uncertain place,
ask for the Alcayde of Sheftheim.
A fox will show you the bridle-path, follow,
the music of the oak will be your fitting welcome.
Let the wilderness close behind you.
From here on no compass, only open senses.

89

To rise with the morning mist
on Lake Silvaplana and to disintegrate
as triumphant iridescence on the icy peaks.
Called near Capernaum to walk
with sun and moon, falling back
as a drop of blood into Mary the Mother's cloak.
To drink the last drink from the hollowed hand
at the Castalian fountain, to moisten the temples
and vanish wordlessly in the rock. To lie in
my Sheftheim under the oak, to watch the glowworms
and to be sucked up by the roots. For ever.

90

We circle pointlessly, aimlessly, endlessly, Amen.
Imagination may talk a great deal:
He wanted to, ought to have, had, was;
that too will soon sleep in the dark:
Saxifrage on solid magma,
sheet lightning in night and ice.
New fates are jumbled in the shaken bag.
Atoms dance, possibilities swirl,
nothing can be foretold. And your
mystery remains impenetrable: *Lumen mundi.*

1981